# DINOSAURS

Time, Money & Fractions

1. Basic time telling (Hours and half hours)
2. counting amounts of money
3. Understanding fractions

DINOSAUR

Face Clocks: Identifying Parts

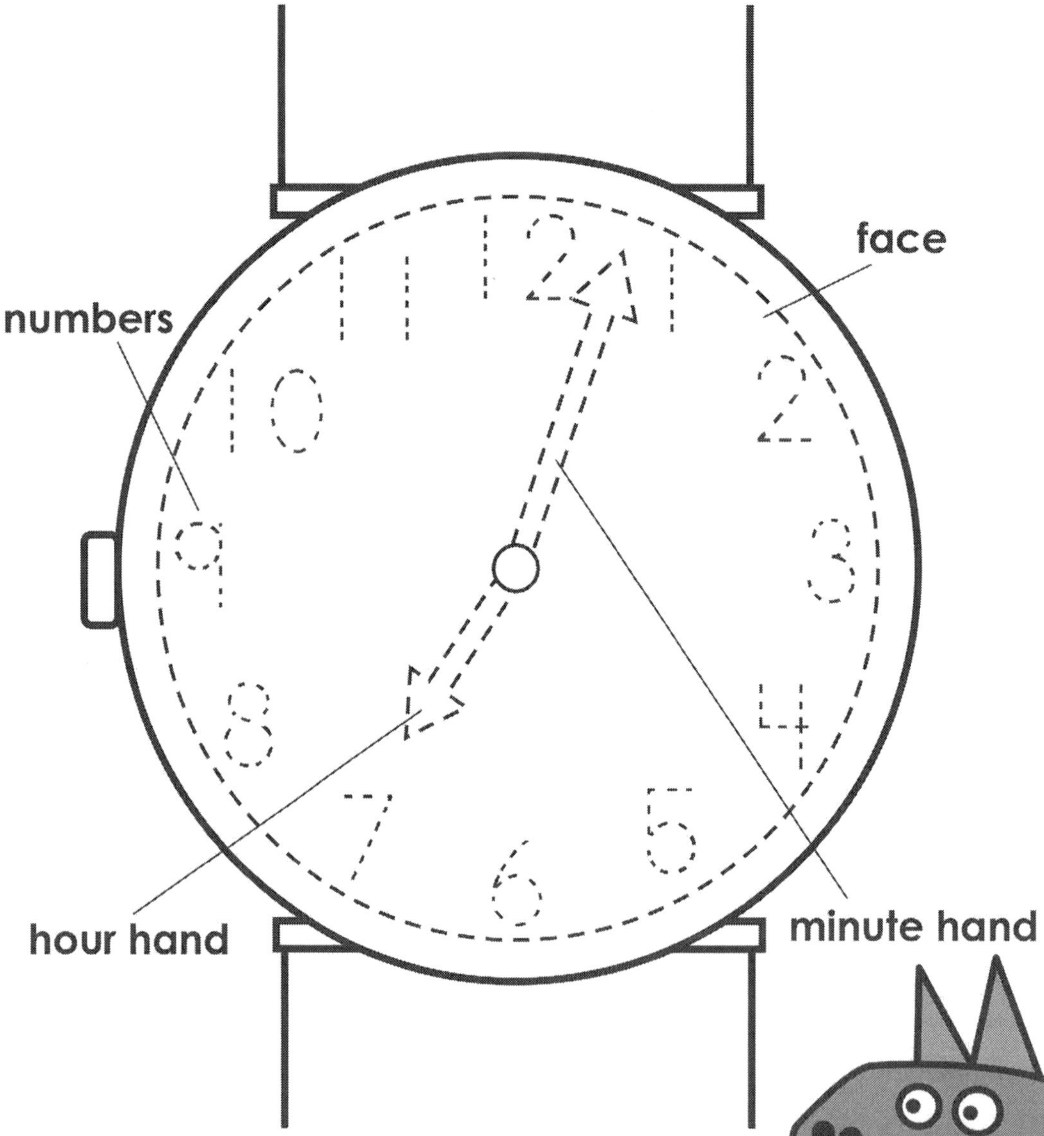

Face Clocks: Identifying Parts

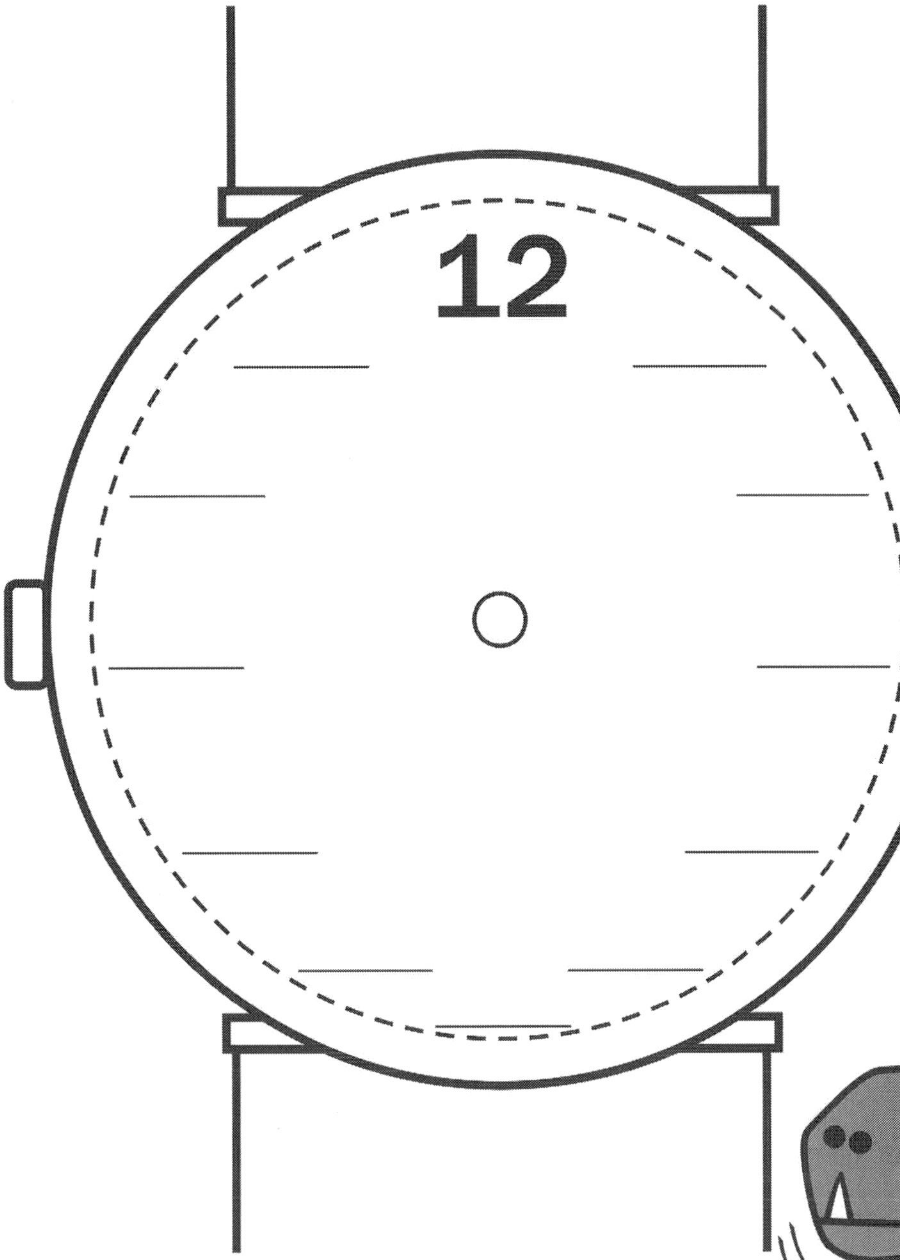

12

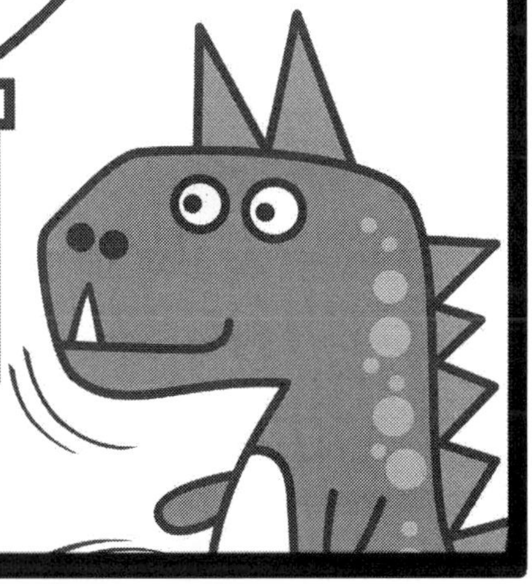

DINOSAUR

HOURS

DINOSAUR

Face Clocks: Introduction

What time it is?

Circle the ones you have seen.

4:00

DINOSAUR

Face Clocks: Introduction
What time it is?
Circle the ones you have seen.

9:00

DINOSAUR

Face Clocks: Introduction

What time it is?
Circle the ones you have seen.

2:00

DINOSAUR

Face Clocks: Introduction

What time it is?
Circle the ones you have seen.

11:00

DINOSAUR

Face Clocks: Introduction

What time it is?

Circle the ones you have seen.

6:00

DINOSAUR

Face Clocks: Introduction

What time it is?
Circle the ones you have seen.

3:00

DINOSAUR

Face Clocks: Introduction

What time it is?
Circle the ones you have seen.

10:00

DINOSAUR

Face Clocks: Introduction

What time it is?
Circle the ones you have seen.

5:00

DINOSAUR

Face Clocks: Introduction

What time it is?
Circle the ones you have seen.

12:00

DINOSAUR

Face Clocks: Introduction

What time it is?
Circle the ones you have seen.

DINOSAUR

Write the Time. Fill in the blanks

The BIG HAND is on ...12......

The little hand is on ......1......

It is ......1...... o'clock

DINOSAUR

Write the Time. Fill in the blanks

The BIG HAND is on...12........

The little hand is on.....4........

It is .....4......o'clock

DINOSAUR

Write the Time. Fill in the blanks

The BIG HAND is on ...12......

The little hand is on ....7........

It is .....7.... o'clock

DINOSAUR

Write the Time. Fill in the blanks

The BIG HAND is on...12........

The little hand is on...10......

It is ...10...o'clock

DINOSAUR

Write the Time. Fill in the blanks

The BIG HAND is on. 12

The little hand is on. 2

It is ....2.... o'clock

DINOSAUR

Write the Time. Fill in the blanks

The BIG HAND is on...12........

The little hand is on....5........

It is ...5......o'clock

DINOSAUR

Circling the Hour Hand

Circle the little hour hand on each clock.

What time is it? Write the time below.

It is ………o'clock

DINOSAUR

Circling the Hour Hand

Circle the little hour hand on each clock.

What time is it? Write the time below.

It is ....6.....o'clock

DINOSAUR

Circling the Hour Hand

Circle the little hour hand on each clock.

What time is it? Write the time below.

It is ......9...... o'clock

DINOSAUR

Circling the Hour Hand

Circle the little hour hand on each clock.

What time is it? Write the time below.

It is ………o'clock

DINOSAUR

Drawing the Hour Hand

Draw the little hour hand on each clock.

11 o'clock

DINOSAUR

Drawing the Hour Hand

Draw the little hour hand on each clock.

7 o'clock

DINOSAUR

Drawing the Hour Hand

Draw the little hour hand on each clock.

5 o'clock

DINOSAUR

Drawing the Hour Hand

Draw the little hour hand on each clock.

2 o'clock

DINOSAUR

Drawing the Hour Hand

Draw the little hour hand on each clock.

4 o'clock

DINOSAUR

Drawing the Hour Hand

Draw the little hour hand on each clock.

12 o'clock

DINOSAUR

What is the time?

10 o klok

DINOSAUR

What is the time?

DINOSAUR

What is the time?

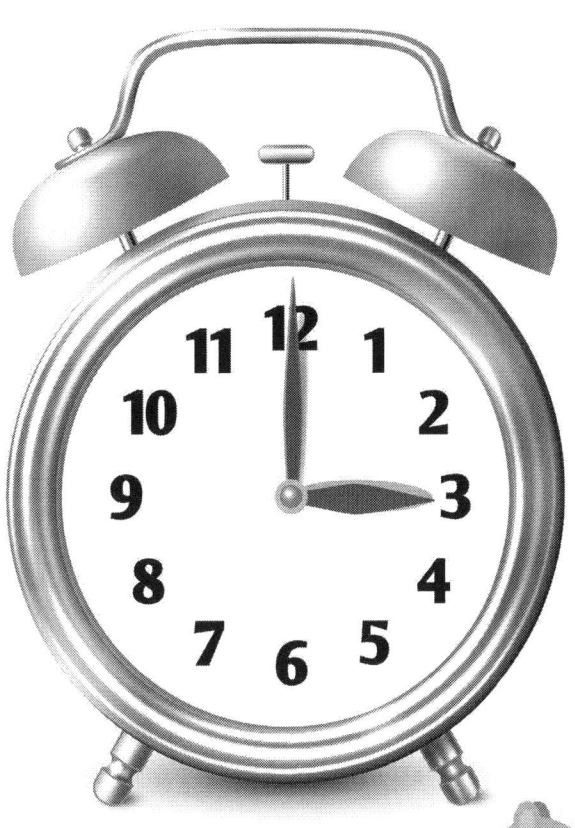
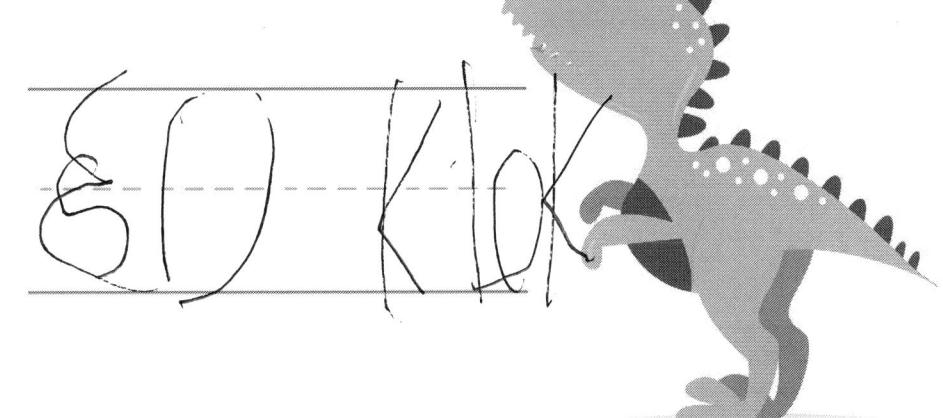

3 o klok

DINOSAUR

What is the time?

7 oklok

DINOSAUR

Face Clocks: Introduction

What time it is?
Circle the ones you have seen.

5:30

DINOSAUR

Face Clocks: Introduction

What time it is?
Circle the ones you have seen.

11:30

DINOSAUR

Face Clocks: Introduction

What time it is?
Circle the ones you have seen.

12:30

DINOSAUR

Face Clocks: Introduction

What time it is?

Circle the ones you have seen.

8:30

DINOSAUR

Face Clocks: Introduction

What time it is?
Circle the ones you have seen.

2:30

DINOSAUR

Face Clocks: Introduction

What time it is?
Circle the ones you have seen.

12:30

DINOSAUR

Face Clocks: Introduction

What time it is?
Circle the ones you have seen.

3:30

DINOSAUR

Face Clocks: Introduction

What time it is?
Circle the ones you have seen.

9:30

DINOSAUR

Face Clocks: Introduction

What time it is?
Circle the ones you have seen.

4:30

DINOSAUR

Face Clocks: Introduction

What time it is?
Circle the ones you have seen.

1:30

DINOSAUR

Write the Time. Fill in the blanks

The BIG HAND is on ......6......

The little hand is on ...4......

It is ...4:30............

DINOSAUR

Write the Time. Fill in the blanks

The BIG HAND is on... 6

The little hand is on... 3

It is ... 3:30

DINOSAUR

Write the Time. Fill in the blanks

The BIG HAND is on...6......

The little hand is on...7......

It is ...7:30............

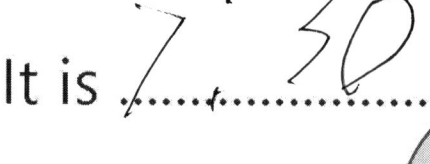

DINOSAUR

Write the Time. Fill in the blanks

The BIG HAND is on... 6

The little hand is on... 10

It is ...

DINOSAUR

Write the Time. Fill in the blanks

The BIG HAND is on… 6

The little hand is on… 6

It is … 6:30

DINOSAUR

Write the Time. Fill in the blanks

The BIG HAND is on............ 6

The little hand is on..............

It is 3:30

DINOSAUR

Circling the Hour Hand

Circle the little hour hand on each clock.

What time is it? Write the time below.

It is 11:30

DINOSAUR

Circling the Hour Hand

Circle the little hour hand on each clock.

What time is it? Write the time below.

It is 8:30

DINOSAUR

Circling the Hour Hand

Circle the little hour hand on each clock.

What time is it? Write the time below.

It is 5:30

DINOSAUR

Circling the Hour Hand

Circle the little hour hand on each clock.

What time is it? Write the time below.

It is ....

DINOSAUR

Circling the Hour Hand

Circle the little hour hand on each clock.

What time is it? Write the time below.

It is ....

DINOSAUR

Circling the Hour Hand

Circle the little hour hand on each clock.

What time is it? Write the time below.

It is 12:30

DINOSAUR

Draw the little hour hand on each clock.

3:30

DINOSAUR

Draw the little hour hand on each clock.

6:30

DINOSAUR

Draw the little hour hand on each clock.

10:30

DINOSAUR

Draw the little hour hand on each clock.

2:30

DINOSAUR

Draw the little hour hand on each clock.

7:30

DINOSAUR

Draw the little hour hand on each clock.

5:30

DINOSAUR

Counting Money

DINOSAUR

Counting Nickels

Count the money. Write the amount.

a.  ~~50~~ ¢

b.  35 ¢

c.
45 ¢

d.
5 ¢

e.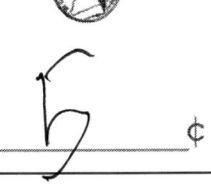
20 ¢

f.
40 ¢

g.
85 ¢

h.
50 ¢

i.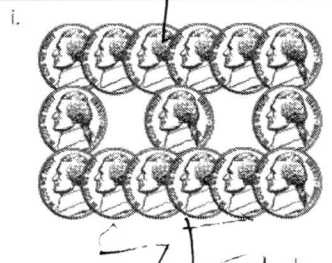
75 ¢

j.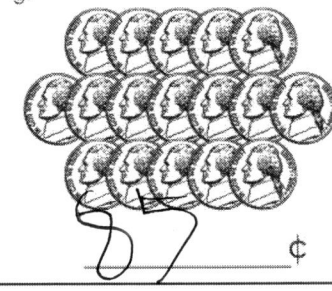
15 ¢

k.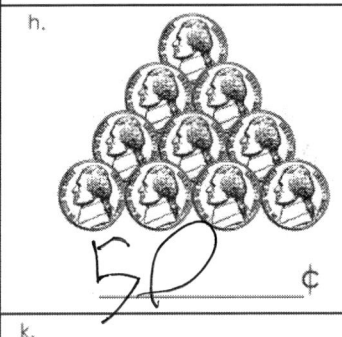
45 ¢

DINOSAUR

ANSWER KEY

Counting Nickels

Count the money. Write the amount.

a. 55 ¢

b. 35 ¢

c. 45 ¢

d. 5 ¢

e. 20 ¢

f. 40 ¢

g. 85 ¢

h. 50 ¢

i. 75 ¢

j. 15 ¢

k. 45 ¢

DINOSAUR

Counting Quarters

Count the money. Write the amount.

A+

a.     1.00 ✓

b.   0.50 ✓

c.
0.25 ✓

d.
1.00 ✓

e.
0.75 ✓

f.
0.50 ✓

g.
0.50 ✓

h.
1.00 ✓

i.
0.75 ✓

j.
1.00 ✓

k.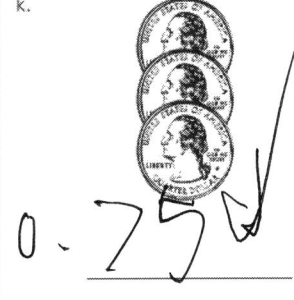
0.75 ✓

DINOSAUR

ANSWER KEY

Counting Quarters

Count the money. Write the amount.

a.     $1.00

b.   $0.50

c.
$0.25

d.
$1.00

e.
$0.75

f.
$0.50

g.
$0.50

h.
$1.00

i.
$0.75

j.
$1.00

k.
$0.75

DINOSAUR

Counting Money

 3 300	 2 200	 0
2 50	 0	 0
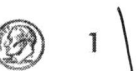 1 10	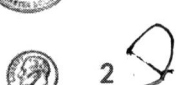 2 20	 2 20
 2 10	 0	 3 15
 0	 8 8	 7 7
How much money in all? 3'70	How much money in all? 2'28	How much money in all? 0.42
 4 400	 1 100	 1 100
 1 25	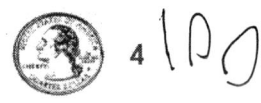 4 100	 1 25
4 40	1 10	5 50
0	 3 15	5 25
4 4	1 1	9 9
How much money in all? 4'69	How much money in all? 2'26	How much money in all? 2'9

DINOSAUR

ANSWER KEY
Counting Money

$1: 3	$1: 2	$1: 0
Quarter: 2	Quarter: 0	Quarter: 0
Dime: 1	Dime: 2	Dime: 2
Nickel: 2	Nickel: 0	Nickel: 3
Penny: 0	Penny: 8	Penny: 7

How much money in all?

$3.70 $2.28 $0.42

$1: 4	$1: 1	$1: 1
Quarter: 1	Quarter: 4	Quarter: 1
Dime: 4	Dime: 1	Dime: 5
Nickel: 0	Nickel: 3	Nickel: 5
Penny: 4	Penny: 1	Penny: 9

How much money in all?

$4.69 $2.26 $2.09

DINOSAUR

Fraction of a Group

Color the fraction listed for each group.

a.

$$\frac{3}{6}$$

b.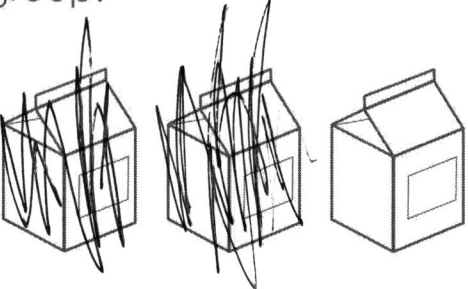

$$\frac{2}{3}$$

c.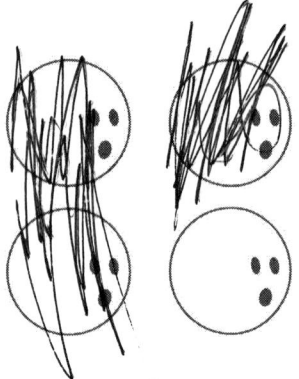

$$\frac{3}{4}$$

d.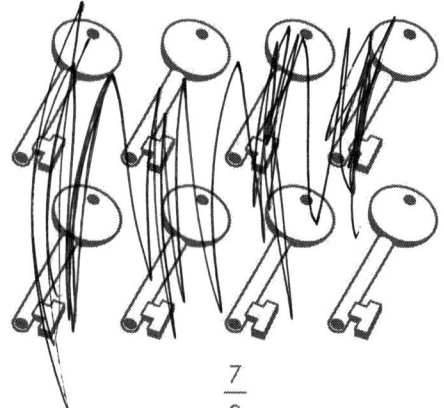

$$\frac{7}{8}$$

e.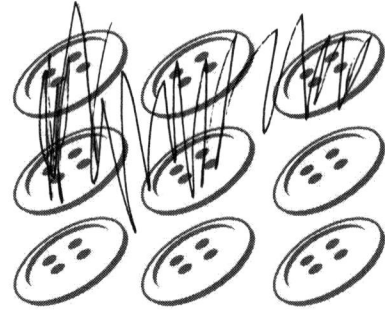

$$\frac{5}{9}$$

f.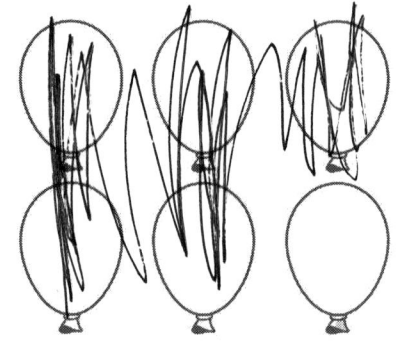

$$\frac{5}{6}$$

DINOSAUR

ANSWER KEY

Fraction of a Group

Color the fraction listed for each group.

a.

$\frac{3}{6}$

b.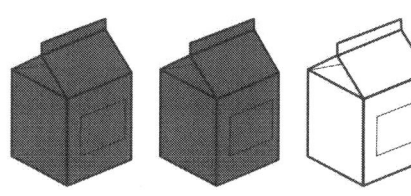

$\frac{2}{3}$

c.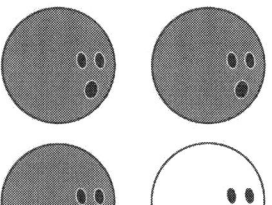

$\frac{3}{4}$

d.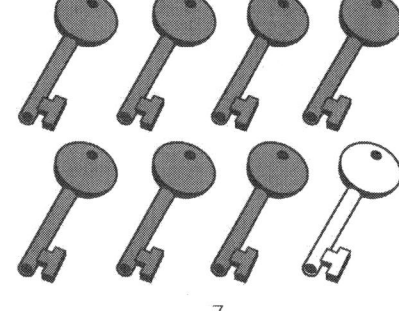

$\frac{7}{8}$

e.

$\frac{5}{9}$

f.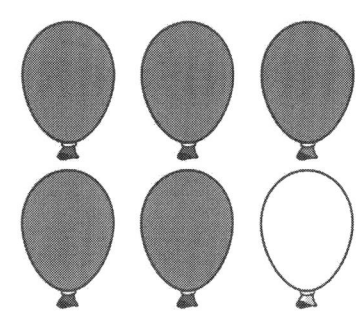

$\frac{5}{6}$

DINOSAUR

Fractions

Tell what fraction of each shape is shaded.

a. 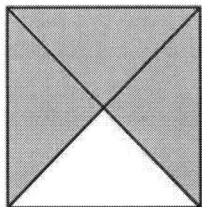 b. 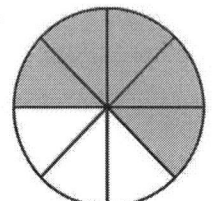 c.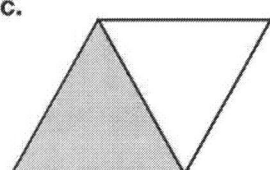

d. 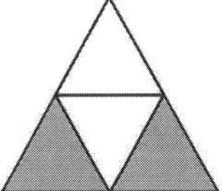 e. 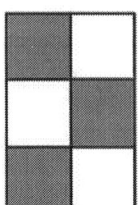 f.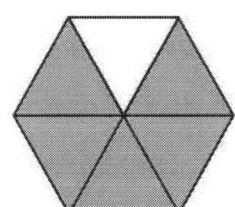

g. 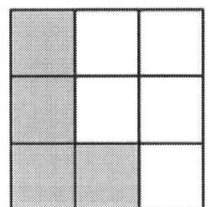 h. 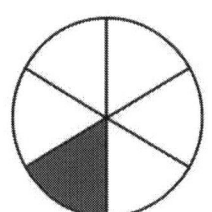 i.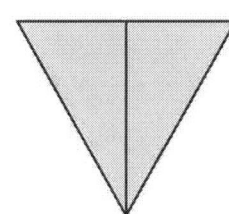

j. 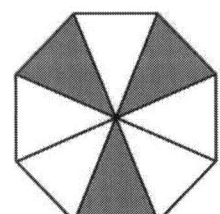 k. 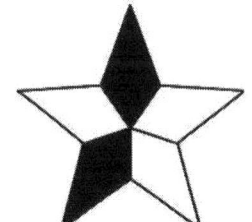 l.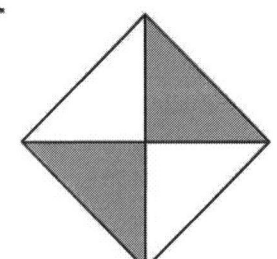

DINOSAUR

ANSWER KEY
Fractions

Tell what fraction of each shape is shaded.

a.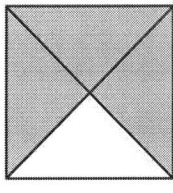
$\frac{3}{4}$

b.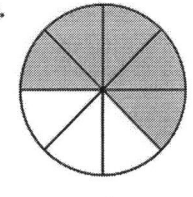
$\frac{5}{8}$

c.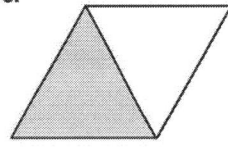
$\frac{1}{2}$

d.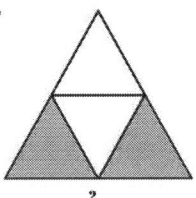
$\frac{2}{4}$

e.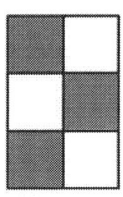
$\frac{3}{6}$

f.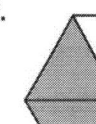
$\frac{5}{6}$

g.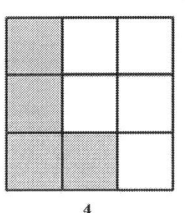
$\frac{4}{9}$

h.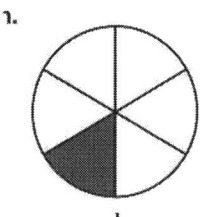
$\frac{1}{6}$

i.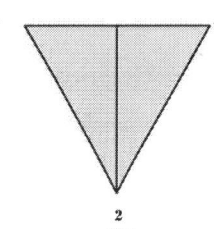
$\frac{2}{2}$

j.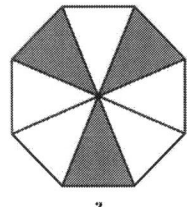
$\frac{3}{8}$

k.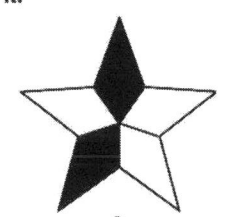
$\frac{2}{5}$

l.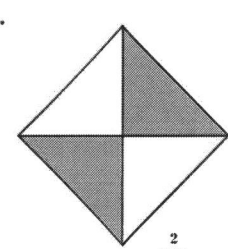
$\frac{2}{2}$

Kids' Activity Workbook Subscribe

Get New Update, Book Giveaway, Free Book for Kids and Promotion

http://bit.ly/act_book_4_kids

MORE KIDS' ACTIVITY BOOKS FROM US
https://k-imagine-pub.com/

K IMAGINE EDUCATION © 2018. All rights reserved.

No part of this publication may be reproduced, distributed, or transmitted in any form or by any means, including photocopying, recording, without the prior written permission of the publisher

Made in the USA
Monee, IL
23 January 2025

10750037R00044